1	Musing at the Museum
4	The Poetry of Hangzhou
8	The Sound of Hangzhou
13	Hungry Hangzhou
14	Hangzhou's Greatest Foodies
18	Signature Hangzhou Dishes
23	Longjing Shrimp
27	Eat Well on Royal Streets
32	For the Family
33	We Are Family
39	Road Trip
43	Making Hangzhou Home
46	Staying Centered and Keeping Fit
51	Take It as Read
53	Traditional Chinese Medicine in Hangzhou
55	Appendix

专业外教　英文朗读
扫码免费收听全书

更多英文原创中国故事
来《汉语世界》畅读
theworldofchinese.com

注册网站，点击右上角 subscribe 订阅，
输入优惠码 HANGZHOU
享受读者专属折扣！

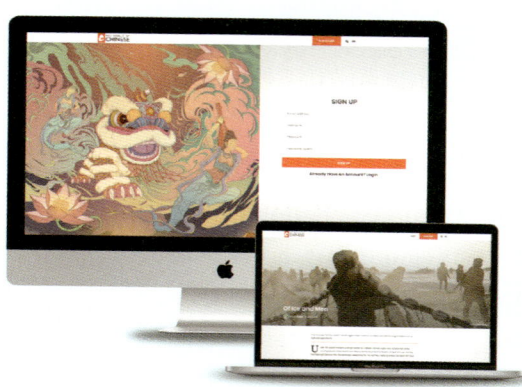

Musing at the Museum

The history and natural beauty of Hangzhou have made it a center for some of the world's finest artistic achievements. Be it copper sculpture or Chinese opera, the people of Hangzhou have been at the forefront of the art world for centuries, creating forms and methods that last even today. Tomorrow's artists, too, are being created in the city of Hangzhou, where the China Academy of Art (CAA), China's first and possibly finest art institution, has set down roots.

There are plenty of museums and galleries to keep you interested and entertained. It's also worth keeping in mind that four of the great ink-painting masters—Feng Zikai, Zhang Daqian, Huang Binhong and Pan Tianshou—are all to a greater or lesser extent linked with Hangzhou and its history. This city of poets and philosophers has been home to some of China's greatest art movements, and the fact that Hangzhou is home to the China Academy of Art means that this legacy will continue far into the future.

muse
沉思

forefront
最前列

ink-painting
水墨画

fanatic
狂热者

layman
外行

staple
主要部分

Pritzker Prize
普利兹克建筑奖

echo
再现

aesthetics
美学

Zhejiang Art Museum

If you're not an art fanatic yet, go to Zhejiang Art Museum to get started. Opened in 2009, Zhejiang Art Museum was built for the layman, where people from all over the world can get to know the nation's art history. A great deal of emphasis (and explanation) is put on traditional Chinese cultural staples like classic paintings, calligraphy, traditional sculpture, folk arts, and handicrafts.

China Academy of Art, Xiangshan Campus

The stunning buildings at Xiangshan Campus at the CAA are masterpieces of Wang Shu, dean of the CAA School of Architecture as well as the first Chinese citizen to win the Pritzker Prize. Wang's buildings are bravely experimental and echo traditional Chinese architecture, especially the aesthetics of classic gardens and ancient academies. The campus is an ambitious attempt to establish a new Chinese architectural aesthetic, and a very successful one at that. Other than the architecture, the campus also has a wide variety of exhibition spaces, museums, and galleries that display all kinds of art.

CAA Art Museum

For young artists in China, Hangzhou is heaven. The CAA Art Museum is at the main campus of China Academy of Art, whose prestige gives the museum a rich collection of established modern artists. The museum is practically a hall-of-fame for China's greatest artists, but it also features the latest works of China's best up-and-comers who are using Hangzhou as a lens for their genius. Of course, the best part of the CAA is that it's surrounded by all those minor galleries that make a day in the district worth having. A nice stroll down Nanshan Road will give you everything you need to know about the state of art and culture in China today.

Pan Tianshou Memorial

Pan Tianshou, one of the most important traditional Chinese painters of the 20th century, laid a foundation for Chinese painting education at a time when Western painting techniques had a tremendous influence. Like his teacher, Wu Changshuo, he applied the aesthetics of calligraphy and seal-carving to his paintings but injected dynamism into his powerful brushstrokes. You can see Pan's representative works at the memorial and read about his tumultuous life.

---

hall-of-fame
名人纪念馆

up-and-comer
有潜力的人

tremendous
巨大的

dynamism
活力

tumultuous
动荡的

The Poetry of Hangzhou

West Lake is often considered the soul of Hangzhou, and, as such, poets have found its shores a perfect setting for their musings for centuries. Many of the lake's famous sites make appearances in works of poetry throughout the ages.

Bai Juyi and His Lady West Lake

Bai Juyi, a poet of the Tang Dynasty, was the three-year governor of Hangzhou; of his poems, more than 200 were about West Lake, making him perhaps the most prolific West Lake poet in history. Upon his departure, he wrote "Why can't I leave Hangzhou easily? West Lake is half the reason." Bai was also the first to explicitly characterize the lake as feminine. In his works, things like women's belts and eyebrows were all metaphors for the lake, eventually earning the body of water the title, "Lake of Beauties."

The Hermit's Hangzhou

Though not as famous as Bai Juyi, Lin Bu made his mark on the ancient

---

prolific
多产的

explicitly
明确地

literary scene with his love of West Lake. A poet of the Northern Song Dynasty, Lin Bu retired to Hangzhou to become a hermit. His poem "West Lake" states: "The water in the spring is clearer than a monk's eyes; and the color of the mountains are as green as the head of the Buddha." Lin, unlike many poets of his day, stayed away from the mundane, earthly aesthetics of poetry. Never marrying, it was said that the cranes of the rivers were his children and the plum blossoms of the land his wife.

mundane
世俗的

smear
涂抹

fancy
魅力

apt
恰当的

Su Shi and the Song

During the Song Dynasty, West Lake truly emerged as the subject of pure beauty. Su Shi, one of the most influential poets of the age, was an official in Hangzhou. One of his most popular poems posits a renowned Chinese metaphor. Su wrote: "If you wish to compare the lake in the West to the Lady of the West, lightly powdered or thickly smeared, the fancy is just as apt." Xizi referred to Xishi, who ranked first among the renowned Four Beauties of Ancient China, and, like her, Su believed West Lake looked beautiful regardless of season, giving the lake yet another nickname, "Xizi Lake."

brutality
暴行

indulgence
沉溺

evoke
唤起

torment
折磨

Lin Sheng After the Fall

The story of poetry in Hangzhou wasn't all flowers, cranes, and changing seasons. There were dark days as well. After the downfall of the Northern Song Dynasty, the Jin army captured many members of the imperial family. Continuous attacks from the Jin army meant that the newly installed regime of the Southern Song Dynasty had to flee to Lin'an (currently Hangzhou) and officially establish it as the capital. While this is considered a golden age of Hangzhou history, the war, destruction, and relocation of the capital were largely regarded as a tragedy. Poet Lin Sheng wrote a famous work criticizing those who forgot the brutalities of history for the indulgences of Hangzhou's beauty: "Peaks rise beyond peaks, and towers on towers. The songs and dances on West Lake proceed into the night. The warm breeze makes everyone drunk, so they think of Hangzhou as the old capital Bianzhou." The poem evokes emotions regarding Hangzhou's tormented history; the haven of Hangzhou came at a cost.

Poetry Built on General Yue and Faithful Yu

Yuan Mei, a poet of the Qing Dynasty, focused his pen on historic figures. In his work "Paying Homage to the Temple of Yue Fei," he wrote: "It is because the two officials Yue Fei and Yu Qian are buried here that people began to value West Lake." Yue Fei, a general of the Southern Song Dynasty, fought a harsh campaign against the invading Jurchens in an effort to retake northern China, which was occupied by the Jin Dynasty in 1126. Yue, nearing victory, was framed by corrupt officials and recalled by the emperor, imprisoned and executed on false charges. Yu Qian had a very similar fate as Yue, though in the Ming Dynasty. Born in Hangzhou, Yu became an official. He led the military to protect the capital against the Mongols and won, but was falsely accused of treason and executed. Both men are reminders that the inspiration of West Lake came from great leaders as well as its natural beauty.

---

homage
致敬

Jurchen
女真族

frame
陷害

Mongol
蒙古人

treason
谋反

The Sound of Hangzhou

Hangzhou has a variety of choices for opera lovers. If you like listening to gentle melodies and watching some classic Chinese romances, then Yue opera is probably your best bet—with its easy-to-follow story lines and pleasant tones. Also in Hangzhou, you can also pick up some Kunqu opera—classified by UNESCO as an intangible cultural heritage.

Yue Opera

Originating from Zhejiang's Sheng County in the late Qing Dynasty, femininity is a major feature of Yue Opera, and male roles are often taken by female performers. Artists from around the country would come to craft scripts for this medium, the most well-known of which are "Butterfly Lovers," "Dream of the Red Chamber," and "The Story of the Western Wing." With its over 100 years history, Yue opera is still popular today, especially in Zhejiang Province and Shanghai. If you're not sure if Yue opera is for you, Huanglongdong Park is a good place

---

Yue opera
越剧

Kunqu opera
昆曲

craft script
创作剧本

wing
厢房

to start. It features 20-minute shows throughout the day. Another reason to start here is because they're frequented by older opera fans who will be happy to walk you through the more difficult bits.

Kunqu Opera

As one of the oldest forms of the art, Kunqu opera is known as the "father of all Chinese operas." Originating from Kunshan, Jiangsu Province, Kunqu evolved from local Kunshan melodies. Combining drama, traditional dance, poetry, and music, it became popular in the Ming Dynasty and has had 600 years history. Although Kunqu is older and less popular than Peking opera, the two have several things in common, including the structure of the cast: a female lead, a male lead, a comic role, and an elderly man.

The major musical instrument in Kunqu opera is China's traditional horizontal bamboo flute (or *dizi* in Chinese). Representative works of Kunqu opera are "The Peony Pavilion," "Peach Blossom Fan," and "The Story of the Western Wing." In 2001, UNESCO declared Kunqu opera a "masterpiece

Peking opera
京剧

cast
全体演员

female lead
女主角

fine dining	高级餐饮
playwright	剧作家
obsession	痴迷
nocturnal tryst	夜间幽会
bewitch	施魔法于
novice	新手
conjure up	召唤

of the oral and intangible heritage of humanity."

The Peony Pavilion

There are few better ways to spend an evening in Hangzhou than in the elegant settings, where you can enjoy some fine dining and watch the famed Kunqu opera "The Peony Pavilion" in one of the city's most attractive historical blocks.

"The Peony Pavilion" was penned by Tang Xianzu, who was the Ming court's official playwright. Without spoiling the story too much, the opera centers on the 16-year-old Du Liniang's love affair with a young scholar Liu Mengmei. After falling in love with the young man (who she has never actually met) in a vivid dream, the maiden becomes lovesick and develops an unhealthy obsession with her nocturnal tryst. Falling severely ill, the girl dies from a broken heart, only to be brought back to life by the lord of the underworld after visiting and bewitching the young scholar in his dreams.

Even for the opera novices out there, it's hard not to be completely swept away by this highly exciting experience, and the atmosphere conjured up by the actors, the musicians, and the wonderful set design is so thick you could cut it with a knife. The small group of musicians who accompany the play—all dressed in traditional garb and clutching traditional instruments—also impress with their delicate playing and nuanced musical sensitivity. All in all, this epic tale of delicate romance, reincarnation, and bittersweet love is something that will stay with you long after the final curtain falls.

Theaters

As with many elements of the city, the performance scene in Hangzhou strikes a balance between the modern and the traditional. Pop singers and bands gravitate toward Dragon Sports Center for their concerts, so that area is more for the younger crowd. You'll find a very different vibe at the Hangzhou Grand Theatre, which is a landmark architectural feat and the largest theater in Hangzhou. Many different shows—domestic and foreign, traditional and modern—are held here, and it remains the top choice for opera directors and musicians who want to showcase their work in Hangzhou. It isn't all rarefied theater performances; it also regularly stages quality children's plays.

garb
装束

clutch
紧握

nuanced
有细微差别的

reincarnation
转世

gravitate
被吸引

feat
壮举

rarefied
高深的

dazzling
眩目的

transcend
超越

Impression West Lake

A feast of music, dance, sound and light effects, "Impression West Lake" is a poetic open-air performance during summer time. With Zhang Yimou among its directors and Kitaro as its composer, the five-act show is based on local folklores and legends including the "Legend of the White Snake" and the "Butterfly Lovers." Now the show has received a full upgrade that will definitely leave you with a deep impression of West Lake and the city.

Romance of the Song Dynasty

Like the "O Show" of Las Vegas or "Moulin Rouge" of Paris, "Romance of the Song Dynasty" is a must-see when you are in Hangzhou. This panoramic show hosted by Song Dynasty Town, the Song Dynasty theme park on Zhijiang Road, presents the history of Hangzhou from the dawn of civilization to the modern day, complete with splendid dance, music, and effects. The dazzling Southern Song court performance, the heroic and tragic life story of General Yue Fei, the legendary lady of the West—the stories of the city are on full display in a way that transcends language and culture.

Hungry Hangzhou

In the well-ordered cosmos of Chinese cuisine types, the Zhejiang culinary system plays counterpart to the searing Sichuan peppercorns and the daring appetites of the Cantonese. As the system's most famous representative, Hangzhou cuisine embodies all the best qualities of its namesake city. There is an emphasis on fresh ingredients, inspiration from local history, a delicate presentation, and a Confucian harmoniousness in the classification and balancing of flavors. Even the profusion of steamed and boiled dishes is perhaps a nod to the watery Hangzhou environment and humid weather. Whether it is braised pork named after a poet or cake made with the perfumed petals of the official city flower, the osmanthus, Hangzhou cuisine is irresistibly charming. And who can forget the famous Longjing tea grown right here on the southern slopes of West Lake? There's something for everyone in this centuries-old culinary paradise.

culinary
烹饪的

searing
灼热的

daring
大胆的

Cantonese
广东人

namesake
同名的

Confucian
儒家的

profusion
丰富

humid
潮湿的

braise
炖

petal
花瓣

osmanthus
桂花

irresistibly
无法抵抗地

Hangzhou's Greatest Foodies

First-timers to Hangzhou often think at first that the food is a bit bland. Rather than concentrating on the overly-seasoned diet, Hangzhou cuisine places an emphasis on qualities such as freshness, natural flavors, and respect for the food's unique texture.

The poets and scholars that seemed to gravitate to Hangzhou naturally became the city's food critics. A list of China's great foodies of the past includes Su Shi, Lin Hong, Li Yu, and Yuan Mei—each with an influential recipe book under their name that is still cherished by modern Chinese cooks. Every one of them cultivated their taste buds in Hangzhou.

Although they lived in different times, these great poet-cooks shared many of the same values on food as the foodies of today. They studied natural flavor and texture, used restraint in seasoning, abstained from lavishness in presentation, and they even rejected cruel farming techniques. The local cuisine of Hangzhou is identified by the careful, delicate art of making food with the care of a poet.

---

foodie
美食家

bland
清淡的

texture
口感

gravitate to
倾向于

restraint
克制

abstain
避免

lavishness
过度

Su Shi and Pork

Su Shi, the respected 11th century poet and Hangzhou governor, more popularly known for his pen name Dongpo Jushi, is the inventor of the dish "Dongpo" pork.

Dongpo pork involves pan-frying a chunk of pork belly with a fatty layer. It is then boiled on low heat with soy sauce, sugar, fermented bean paste, and Shaoxing wine until it is tender, almost falling apart. Su Shi, a lover of pork, even wrote a poem on cooking pork: "Mild is the fire, shallow is the water, give it time, and it will be divine." Literally meaning "Dongpo Meat," the dish sounds a bit cannibalistic to some, and 600 years later food critic Li Yu was still making fun of this observation in the pork section of his own recipe book: "What had he done to feed his flesh to hungry people for hundreds of years? I know how to appreciate pork, but I do not dare to say a word about it for fear that I become the second Dongpo."

Less Meat, More Vegetables

Lin Hong, a scholar of the 12th century who spent his prime years in a Hangzhou prison, was the author of *Pure

fermented
已发酵的

cannibalistic
同类相食的

expound
阐述

sage
智者

frugal
俭朴的

mediocre
平庸的

Supplies of the Mountain People, a recipe book that mainly consisted of vegetarian dishes.

Li Yu, a script writer and opera theorist who lived between the Ming and Qing dynasties, was another strong vegetarian advocate. The first sentence of the "Meat" section of his recipe book is, "Meat eaters are base." This, confusing as it is, is a quote from Confucius, and "meat eaters" in the original context meant rulers. Li expounded on the sage's words in his own (not so reliable) way, "Meat eaters are base not because they eat meat but because they are short-sighted. The grease of the meat cools down to solid fat and chokes their chest and heart...Even though I'm writing a recipe for meat, I do advise all my readers: less meat is better." Explaining why he prefers vegetables, Li wrote: "For one, I believe in living a frugal life; for another, we should love all kinds of life and be particularly careful with anything that involves killing."

Beware the Mediocre Cook

Yuan Mei's *Menu of Sui Garden* is perhaps the most widely-read ancient recipe book of its kind. Chefs and food critics are often accused of having eccentric dispositions, and, for his part, Yuan never softened words when discussing his most hated enemy: "the mediocre cook."

"Each food has a flavor of its own, and you can't mingle different flavors. I notice how mediocre cooks put chicken, duck, pork, and goose into one pot to stew…If these animals were aware of it, they would be petitioning for the chef's punishment in hell," Yuan wrote. "Mediocre cooks always keep a pot of pork oil, and finishing each dish with a spoonful, so as to make it greasy. Even the delicate bird's nests are not spared from this humiliation. Those ignorant commoners…are the reincarnations of hungry ghosts."

Yuan's definition of good food, which can still be found in most Hangzhou cuisine today, was balance: "Good food is rich and aromatic, but not greasy; fresh and natural, but not bland."

eccentric
古怪的

disposition
性情

mingle
混合

petition
请愿

commoner
平民

aromatic
有香味的

Signature Hangzhou Dishes

West Lake Carp in Sweet and Sour Sauce

This dish brings together the light flavors of carp and the sweet-and-sour sauce flavors for which Chinese cuisine has become so famous. As with many Chinese dishes, there is a story behind the meal. In this case, an evil official murdered a man so he could be with the dead man's wife. Instead, the wife fled town with her husband's brother, determined to avoid falling into the clutches of the evil official. It is said that on that tragic night when they fled, she cooked this dish as both a reward and farewell for her dead husband's brother. The story, though, has a happy ending: the dead man's brother became a powerful official himself and avenged his brother's death. But hey, when you have some tasty carp ahead of you, a happy ending is all but guaranteed anyway. In addition to a splash of Shaoxing wine, the dish also includes ginger and soy, which give it a full-bodied flavor, and, depending on the chef's preferences, it includes vinegar and sugar in varying quantities.

---

clutch
抢夺

avenge
为……复仇

full-bodied
浓郁的

Beggar's Chicken

A regular on Hangzhou's lists of famous dishes, beggar's chicken consists of chicken wrapped in lotus leaf, with a dab of Shaoxing wine to give it extra flavor. Traditionally, it was roasted in mud, though today this step isn't strictly necessary. In bygone eras, this chicken is said to have been cooked at campfires by lowly beggars who could only wrap their chicken in mud and leaves. Surprisingly, the scent proved delightful, strengthening this dish's place as a must-have for lovers of Hangzhou cuisine. Today, top notch restaurants continue to use clay to separate this dish from other chicken pretenders (though modern chefs first wrap the chicken in cellophane and have perfected the use of safe clays). The end result is a chicken you can literally crack open, to reveal the feast within, and the chicken is often stuffed with other tasty ingredients like shiitake mushrooms.

Black Crab in Egg Yolk

With West Lake hogging all the limelight, it's easy to forget that Hangzhou is just 60 kilometers from the sea. The black crab, or "mud crab," is a crustacean that lives in the shallow

---

lotus leaf
荷叶

a dab of
少许

bygone
很久以前的

campfire
篝火

top notch
一流的

pretender
冒牌货

cellophane
玻璃纸

shiitake mushroom
香菇

hog
独占

limelight
聚光灯

crustacean
甲壳纲动物

Vocabulary	
delta	三角洲
slather	厚厚地涂
brine	盐水
cornstarch	玉米淀粉
gravy	肉汁
simmer	煨炖
savory	好吃的
broth	高汤
crock pot	砂锅

waters of river deltas and sea shores. Hangzhou locals fry and slather them in a sauce made from salty egg yolk. To prepare, take a salted egg that has been soaked in brine, remove the yolk, and crush it to a powder. Keeping the crab in its shell, coat it lightly in cornstarch and fry it in oil until cooked, then remove it from the pan. Mix the egg yolk in the pan with the crab gravy until it becomes a paste. Put the crab back in the pan, coat it in the sauce, and season with cooking wine, red peppers, onion, and ginger.

Immortal Duck and Ham

Searing temperatures followed by a steady simmer are what give this Hangzhou classic dish its signature texture and savory broth. A whole duck is boiled in a covered crock pot at a high temperature together with authentic Jinhua ham, ginger, and green onion, then simmered on low heat for about two hours. The ham is then sliced and placed over the duck. Everything is seasoned with salt and cooking wine and put to simmer for another five minutes before serving. Unfortunately, this dish is falling out of fashion and can be hard to find. However, a similar dish with ham, duck, and Chinese cabbage, called ham and duck hotpot is served at most quality restaurants in the city.

Osmanthus Jelly Cake

Osmanthus cakes are the *xiaolongbao* of desserts: every city has its own recipe. But Hangzhou has them all beat by having an annual festival for appreciating these soft, sweet-scented pastries. Early autumn each year, visitors descend on West Lake and gardens around Hangzhou to view the osmanthus flowers in bloom. It's tradition to set up a table under a fragrant tree and drink Longjing tea, play cards, and eat osmanthus cakes with friends. Legend has it that a scholar brought the flowers to earth from the moon palace, and a peddler who smelled the flowers from outside the scholar's window had the idea of mixing flower petals in the honey-flavored cakes that he sold. You can buy a box at the traditional dessert shops in Hangzhou, and from vendors at Manjuelong Village south of West Lake.

Xiaolongbao

There is no feeling quite like picking up a fresh, soup-filled dumpling about

pastry
糕点

peddler
小贩

vendor
摊贩

mince
剁碎

saturation
饱和

to burst out of its skin. And while it's a big wide world of dumplings out there, *xiaolongbao* can't be beat. Literally "small steam-basket buns," *xiaolongbao* is not your average dumpling. This type of bun bears the typical characteristics of Jiangnan cuisine, boasting intricate folds, a delicate size, a soft yet juicy texture, and an incredible explosion of exciting flavors. Whether it's pork, bamboo shoots, or shrimp, the filling is always minced to ensure softness and saturation, so the sensation of eating a *xiaolongbao* is enriched by its extremely creamy texture.

Hangzhou's homegrown Gan Qi Shi restaurant chain, which claims to sell 20,000 buns per day, opened up a store in Harvard Square in Hangzhou's sister city, Boston. Operating under the name Tom's BaoBao, owner Tom Tong has unveiled to the Boston Globe his ambition to open up 20 to 30 new locations in the next five years and give this typical Chinese food a visibility comparable to hamburgers, the "iconic American food."

A HOME IN HANGZHOU

Longjing Shrimp

Longjing shrimp, a signature dish in Hangzhou cuisine, can bring great pleasure to your dining experience.

The story of Longjing shrimp relates to the Emperor Qianlong, a Qing Dynasty emperor known for his obsession with the southern region and food. On an excursion to the South, Qianlong passed Hangzhou, the hometown of Longjing tea, while touring the picturesque West Lake. Disguised as a commoner, the Emperor hid from the rain in a woman's house and was offered tea made from freshly picked tea leaves boiled in spring water on a charcoal fire. Impressed by the taste but not wanting to reveal his true identity, the emperor pocketed some leaves and continued his trip. At sunset, he reached an inn and ordered several dishes, and among them was fried shrimp. When the emperor passed the tea leaves to the waiter to make some tea, the waiter caught a glimpse of the imperial gown underneath and rushed to inform the chef. Horrified and under immense pressure, the chef accidentally added tea leaves into the dish, mistaking them for green onions. The pink color of the shrimp with the green leaves,

---

signature dish
招牌菜

excursion
远足

picturesque
如画的

disguised as
装扮成

charcoal
木炭

green onion
葱

amino acid
氨基酸

kill off
消灭

kidney
肾脏

circulation
循环

delicacy
美味佳肴

coupled with the fragrance of Longjing, won the emperor over. Thus this classic Hangzhou dish was born.

Consisting mainly of fresh shrimp, the dish is perfect for summer. Rich in amino acids, Longjing tea lowers the body's temperature and kills off bacteria. The river shrimp can strengthen the kidneys and improve circulation. In the *Compendium of Materia Medica*, river shrimp, when peeled and served with ginger and vinegar on the side, are praised as a "delicacy among food."

Longjing shrimp, one of the dishes that Premier Zhou Enlai prepared for President Nixon in Hangzhou during Nixon's visit to China in 1972, has become a classic Hangzhou dish that you simply must try.

Ingredients

20g salt

20g vinegar

5g cornstarch

5g yellow rice wine

1kg river shrimp

25g Longjing tea leaves

500ml cooking oil

50ml hot water

Steps

1. Chill the shrimps for 30 minutes and peel them. Make a pot of tea and let it sit for 15 minutes. Pour the tea into a bowl to soak the peeled shrimp. Add 15 grams of salt, and let it sit for about 20 minutes.

2. Wash the soaked shrimp in water for 20 minutes and use a towel to dry them. In a bowl, add 2 grams of salt and 5 grams of wet cornstarch. Stir until the shrimp are evenly coated.

3. Heat the wok on a high heat and pour in 500 milliliters of cooking oil. Heat until the oil reaches 120 degrees Celsius. Pour the shrimp into the hot oil, stir for 10 seconds, and then fish them out.

4. Add three to four teaspoons of tea, salt, cornstarch, and then put the shrimp back in the wok. Flip four to five times and then plate the shrimp. Decorate the pile with tea leaves and serve.

chill
冷藏

soak
浸泡

wok
炒锅

Celsius
摄氏

teaspoon
茶匙

flip
翻转

杭州一瞥：心灵家园

Eat Well on Royal Streets

In its historical heyday, more than 50,000 people flocked to Qinghefang (also known as Hefang Street) for its daily delicacies, handicrafts, silk, glass, porcelain, and jewels. Qinghefang has been the busiest market place in town from as early as the Southern Song Dynasty. It was located on the west of the Southern Song Imperial Street, at the foot of Wushan Hill and outside the walls of the imperial city. Today, those streets are just as (if not more) busy.

"Everywhere you turn, there are tea houses, wine stores, noodle shops, stalls for snacks, colorful silk, scented candles, condiments, grain, fish, and meat, fresh and preserved," Wu Zimu wrote of the markets in Lin'an during the 13th century in *A Record of the Millet Dream*. On the Southern Song Imperial Street, history lovers are treated to a glass-encased, protected area of the original road. Hefang and the streets nearby contain many wonderful restaurants that will take you back to the dawn of the Southern Song. If you can't find something to eat on Hefang, you won't find it anywhere else.

---

heyday
全盛时期

flock
聚集

porcelain
瓷器

scented
有香味的

condiment
调味品

encased
包住的

hearty
丰盛的

pickle
泡菜

Empress Dowager
皇太后

dry cure
干腌

Jing Yang Guan

Nothing beats a bowl of hot rice in soup, or *paofan*, as a hearty breakfast for authentic Hangzhouness. Pickles, or *jiangcai*, are highlights at any morning table. Jing Yang Guan pickle store was founded in 1907 by 26-year-old Shou Daqing, whose technique was so good that even the royal family couldn't resist this humble folk dish. The pickle's influence in Beijing started with officials from Hangzhou who took their breakfast habits with them when posted to the capital. Before long, everyone, from common northern folk to the Empress Dowager herself, couldn't get enough of Jing Yang Guan's special recipe.

Wanlong Ham House

Noted for its thin skin, tender texture, and limited fat, ham from Jinhua has been considered the best in China for centuries. Dry-cured ham-making techniques have been recorded in this region as far back as the 10th century, and some even claim that Marco Polo took the recipe to Europe. First opened in 1864, this three-story, Western-style building has been carefully preserved and is closely linked to the country's culinary culture. In fact, the Chinese name for "ham" or *huotui*, owes its origins to Jinhua ham. During the Southern Song Dynasty, General Zong Ze and his army passed Jinhua on the way back to the royal court at Hangzhou after a battle with the Jurchen in the north. The locals gave the army salted and dried pork to show their patriotism and support. The general, in turn, offered some to the emperor. Impressed by the taste and touched by the sentiment, the emperor applauded the ham. Seeing the color of the ham as crimson and golden, he named it "flame leg," or *huotui*.

patriotism
爱国心

sentiment
感情

applaud
称赞

crimson
深红色

Jiu Zhi Zhai

Southern pastry is to China pastry what French pastry is to the West pastry. Rich in varieties and tastes, Southern pastry found its opportunity as early as the Song Dynasty and was deeply influenced by the Suzhou style of cooking. Heavy in the use of rose, osmanthus, and orange peels, it's perfect when paired with tea.

First opened in 1925, Jiu Zhi Zhai pastry shop has been a local favorite ever since, but be sure to choose wisely from their seasonal selection: in spring, have

scone 烤饼	a scone with sweet fermented rice wine; in summer, try the green bean cake; in autumn, don't miss the chrysanthemum cake and moon cake; and in winter, try the crunchy sesame candy.
chrysanthemum 菊花	
crunchy 脆的	**Dingsheng Cake**
glutinous rice 糯米	This sweet, pink pastry is a must-have on the historical Hefang Street. Made with glutinous rice and red bean paste, the cake is molded into brick shape with the word "定胜" (*dingsheng*, or definite victory) pressed on it. As for its origin, a legend says that the cake was made by citizens of Lin'an in the Southern Song Dynasty for their soldiers as a token of good luck on the battle field.
red bean paste 红豆沙	
mold 用模子制作	
as a token of 作为……的标志	

Gaoyin Street

Located to the north of Hefang Street, Gaoyin Street is constantly packed with eager locals and curious tourists. Here you can find cuisines from all over China and restaurants that cater to drastically different tastes. Xiao Shao Xin is one of the most popular restaurants on this street. It offers authentic cuisine from the Shaoxing region of Zhejiang Province, and the dish to try there is the shrimp and pork with preserved vegetables; if you're the adventurous sort, try the stinky tofu with minced pork. The famous local franchise Zhi Wei Guan also has one of its high-end restaurants here for visitors wanting a traditional Hangzhou meal. But if you want a break from southern cuisine, head for Dong Yi Shun, which offers Xinjiang cuisine—and you can never get tired of skewers and roasted lamb ribs. And there is Huangfanr, where Emperor Qianlong used to eat on southern tours. For those just looking for a snack, try the fried eel noodles from A Liang Noodle Restaurant.

---

drastically
极其

preserved vegetable
梅干菜

adventurous
富于冒险精神的

stinky tofu
臭豆腐

franchise
连锁店

skewer
烤串

eel
鳝鱼

For the Family

If you find yourself in town with the family in tow, then good for you because Hangzhou has plenty to do for young and old alike. First of all, there are more beautiful spots, cultural attractions, and points-of-interest around town than you can shake a Hello Kitty-brand selfie stick at. From the banks of West Lake to the bustle and hustle of Hefang Street, Hangzhou has much to offer you. Hangzhou's got museums, parks, fairgrounds, zoos, aquariums. You're sure to find people falling over themselves to ensure that you and the little ones have a comfortable, and fun experience in the city that Marco Polo famously described as "heaven on earth."

---

in tow
在一起

selfie stick
自拍杆

bustle and hustle
拥挤喧嚣

fairground
游乐场

aquarium
水族馆

We Are Family

Museums

Top of the list for kid-friendly museums is the Zhejiang Museum of Natural History. Recording the "Life Story of Earth" through a chronologically ordered array of exhibitions, models, interactive displays, and multimedia stations, the museum shows how life on this big blue planet we call home evolved from simple floating organisms that dwelled in the depths of the ocean to the Homo sapiens that walk the streets today.

On the museum's third floor lies an impressive taxidermy collection that includes creatures both great and small, ranging from an African elephant to a tiny frozen-in-time blue tit. Pleasingly, there is also a localized section here that focuses on Zhejiang's own flora and fauna—featuring Zhejiang's 99 species of mammals, 450 different kinds of birds, and 82 species of reptiles native to the province.

Seeing as though you are at the pleasingly futuristic West Lake Cultural Plaza anyway, you can spend an hour or so hanging out and enjoying the well-manicured banks of the Grand Canal, which is the largest man-

---

chronologically
按年代

array
大量

organism
有机体

Homo sapien
智人

taxidermy
动物标本

blue tit
蓝山雀

flora and fauna
动植物群

mammal
哺乳动物

reptile
爬行动物

manicured
修剪整齐的

bask 陶醉	
premier 首要的	
coal barge 运煤船	
stereoscopic 有立体效果的	
do the trick 达到目的	
the Neolithic Age 新石器时代	

made waterway in the world. Here you can bask in the shade of one of the city's premier shopping malls, and watch the large coal barges. Various restaurants and cafes are available both in the plaza's main buildings and in the new underground shopping mall, which boasts a decent food court and a large supermarket.

Museums Around the Lake

Located on Nanshan Road, the West Lake Museum may interest older children, especially if you have already taken them for a good look around the lake. The main hall introduces birds and freshwater fish, as well as relics uncovered from the lake. Visitors can also experience a 3D history lesson in its stereoscopic cinema.

If you want to give your kids real insight into a side of Hangzhou's culture that needs no introduction, then the China National Silk Museum ought to do the trick. Easily accessible by way of Yuhuangshan Road, the museum takes you back to the days of the Qin and Han dynasties and is the largest museum of its kind in China. The museum has eight halls covering everything related to the silk industry—from silkworm cultivation, which dates back 5,000 years to the Neolithic Age to weaving, printing, and dyeing. With accurate English descriptions and interactive video media in each of its halls, this museum is a great way to give your children a taste of the former splendor of China's famed Silk Road.

Taiziwan Park

If you are basing yourself closer to West Lake but fancy a break from the shore-side crowds, then Taiziwan Park, also known as Prince Bay Park, is a fantastic getaway. Located on the northern part of Hupao Road, this park is a popular spot for wedding photography, and it boasts a large wooden windmill that sits majestically at the base of lush hills. When spring hits, this park becomes one of the best spots in town for picnicking or just hanging out. Wander around the park and you'll see all kinds of flowers, especially tulips and cherry trees in full bloom.

Xixi National Wetland Park

Situated in the western part of Hangzhou, and just a few miles from West Lake, the much admired Xixi Wetlands are most definitely worth an afternoon of your time, but in truth you could easily spend a couple of days

fancy
喜爱

windmill
风车

majestically
雄伟地

lush
苍翠茂盛的

tulip
郁金香

sprawling
延展的

blessed with
赋予

exotic
异国的

en-route
在途中

ride
游乐车

rollercoaster
过山车

there. A rare urban wetland that ranks as the "First National Wetland Park in China," Xixi is a sprawling nature reserve blessed with rich ecological resources, simple natural landscapes, and outstanding cultural heritage that includes agricultural life and local history.

The wetlands are a bird-lovers' paradise, and many rare birds and exotic feathered friends stop here en-route to Australia, where they fly from Siberia to escape the harsh winters. Speaking of winters, Hangzhou's coldest months are actually a great time to spot some of the 90-some species that call Xixi their home, so if any of your children are fans of winged wildlife, then the Xixi National Wetland Park is a sure winner.

Hangzhou Paradise

If you and your kids are more into rides and rollercoasters than swans and swallows, then you might want to head in the direction of a few amusement and theme parks. Way out in Hangzhou's southeastern Xiaoshan District is Hangzhou Paradise, which is perhaps the city's oldest and most established amusement park. Separated into a number of different sections, including the Ecological Amusement Park, the Holland Village Theme Park, and the Travels of Marco Polo, this large, slightly manic park touches all the amusement park bases to which we've all become accustomed. The park also includes a large water park that includes a massive wave machine that can create waves that crash in at over one meter high.

Once you've had your fill of paradise, if you've still got the energy, you could take the kids for a stroll around nearby Xianghu Lake. It contains a small beach where you can play sand with your kids by the lake.

Hangzhou Youth & Children's Park

As for places to take the little ones for a couple of hours, Hangzhou Youth & Children's Park is a kind of mini themepark that has numerous children's rides, play areas, a large arcade, and much more. This is all located in a pleasant, shady, tree-filled courtyard that is conveniently situated in the city's bustling center. Kids love this place and it is certainly worth an hour or so of your time if you are in the area and looking for some old-school fun and games.

manic
狂热的

arcade
游乐场

bustling
繁荣的

old-school
复古的

safari 游猎	
traverse 横越	
cheeky 放肆的	
arctic fox 北极狐	
beluga whale 大白鲸	
cetacean 鲸类	
bowhead whale 弓头鲸	

Hangzhou Safari Park

In terms of major parks in Hangzhou that could fill a full day, Hangzhou Safari Park sits right at the top of the list. A zoo that is home to all the animals, Hangzhou's largest safari park is split into two sections, one being a traditional walk-around zoo and the other being a safari park that you can traverse either by "train" or private vehicle. Elephant shows, cheeky flea-picking monkeys, rides for the little ones, and some rather nice lakes and ponds are all on hand here.

Hangzhou Polar Ocean Park

If your kids enjoy the company of animals like polar bears, penguins, and arctic foxes, Hangzhou Polar Ocean Park is a nice place. The best place to see these polar animals is underwater, and the Hangzhou Changqiao Polar Ocean Park has that covered. Perhaps the biggest attraction is the beluga whale exhibit, where visitors can enjoy a large viewing area to watch these curious cetaceans play. Of course, the park is for learning as much as it is for fun; the kids should enjoy the whaling ship and hopefully learn a little bit about the bowhead whale.

Road Trip

If you feel like you've seen enough of Hangzhou and want to take your family on a little road trip, then Hangzhou can be a good base camp from which you can explore some of Zhejiang Province's most interesting counties, towns, and villages. Whether you've rented a car, hired a driver, or feel like taking a trip on China's clean and always-on-time trains, you have a number of options—both near and far—that should put a smile on everyone's face.

If you are keen to explore the delights of the Grand Canal a little deeper, then a short ride to Yuhang District's Tangqi Town could be just what you need. The most eye-catching is Tangqi's crown—Guangji Bridge. At one time Tangqi served as a major transport and trade hub for goods and passengers making their way back and forth between Zhejiang Province and the Ming and Qing capital.

Of particular interest along Tangqi's alleyways and streets is an oil-pressing shop where jars are filled using the traditional method, sending lovely scents

base camp
大本营

alleyway
小巷

oil-pressing
榨油

> **engaging**
> 迷人的

of peanut and sesame oil into the air as local customers watch on. Nearby is a well-protected memorial tablet inscribed with the calligraphy of Hangzhou's favorite emperor, Qianlong.

Well worth the 90-minute or so journey from Hangzhou, is Tonglu County, a scenic wonderland of white clouds, clear brooks, and family-friendly attractions and sights. Built during China's Three Kingdoms Period, Tonglu is a blessed land located on the engaging landscape of the Fuchun River. The town has influenced poets and painters throughout Chinese history with its natural beauty and historic relics, and the beauty and culture of the Fuchun River area has attracted numerous literati, who left behind works of literature and poetry to describe the river landscape.

Well-known as one of China's "Most Beautiful Counties," Tonglu is a great place to unwind for the weekend. Natural riches can be found at virtually every turn. One of the county's main attractions is surely Yaolin Fairyland. Other notable points-of-interest include Daqi Mountain National Forest Park and the Yan Ziling Fishing Platform.

Another place that you really ought to

try and see while you are in this neck of the woods is the Qiandao Lake, a place so beautiful that it makes even the locals go all misty-eyed when mentioned. With numerous picturesque islets, stunning countryside, and unique plants and animals, Chun'an County, as it's known, is truly a sight to visit, and you can easily spend a whole weekend there if you wish to fully immerse yourself in the area's mystical charms. For a bird's eye view of the islets, you can take a cable car to Meifeng Peak. The water here is of the best quality in the whole of China and is used for making bottled water. Located in the Central Lake District, Moonlight Scenic Area is the lake's most famous attraction and comprises five islets connected by three elegant bridges. The Bird Islet has over 6,000 birds representing 50 species, including wading birds, waterfowl, and birds of prey.

Officially part of Greater Hangzhou and situated just 50 minutes from the city's core, Lin'an District boasts a lush landscape that is around 75 percent forest. While the city itself is nothing to write home about, it's the nearby Tianmu Mountain that serves as the area's calling card, along with the

picturesque
图画般的

wade
涉水

bird of prey
猛禽

write home about
值得详述

calling card
标志

outlying 边远的	outlying lakes and forests. The mountain is home to many great scenic spots, gigantic golden cypress trees, and much more that makes it a good option for a beautiful day out in the great outdoors. In terms of its cuisine, Lin'an is known for its fried bamboo shoots and dishes that feature the use of fresh bamboo shoots. Mountain walnuts and chicken-blood stones are also local specialties.
gigantic 巨大的	
cypress 柏树	
glossy 顺滑的	
worm-proof 防虫蛀的	

Located just 35 kilometers from downtown Hangzhou—is a trip to Fuyang District, and particularly to Longmen Ancient Town, which is a perfectly constructed Ming Dynasty town that has a history dating back more than 1,000 years. The native home of Sun Quan, about 65 generations of the Sun family have called Longmen home over the years. The place boasts an amazing labyrinth of complete, ancient buildings and unique Ming and Qing dynasty style. Paper made in Fuyang is regarded as a novelty, known for its glossy and worm-proof texture as well as its pure, white color.

Making Hangzhou Home

When visitors first come to China, they hear all kinds of advice to deal with what can seem confusing. Fortunately, by and large, this doesn't apply to Hangzhou. In Hangzhou, people always have the right-of-way, commuters line up for the subway, and a helping hand is never punished. You'll always find cars ready to stop to let you by at crosswalks. In fact, local drivers will tell you that they've been in the habit of doing so for years, according to a *Zhejiang Daily* report in 2007.

This sort of etiquette extends to those on two wheels as well. To ease traffic congestion and encourage environmentally-friendly transportation, the Hangzhou government invested 180 million RMB into building a public bicycle system which has over 3,500 service spots and 84,000 bicycles operating around the city. All you need to get one is to swipe your transportation card—at the very reasonable rate. Hangzhou boasts one of the largest bike-sharing systems in the world.

But, what is biking if the environment

---

by and large
一般而言

right-of-way
先行权

commuter
通勤者

etiquette
礼仪

congestion
拥堵

swipe
刷

sewage
污水

discharge
排放

sanitary
卫生的

misconduct
不端行为

petition
投诉

is lacking? Conservation is close to the hearts of the people of Hangzhou. The city, for example, has 470 rivers, and in early 2013, according to the Hangzhou Municipal Government, 113 of them were heavily polluted because of illegal sewage discharge. Just two years later, 70 of them have been restored. Even the newspapers play a role in keeping Hangzhou clean. The local bestselling newspaper *Qianjiang Evening Post* has an online platform where photos of sanitary misconduct are posted for public knowledge.

Established in 2010, the office named "Hubin Qingyu" has collected hundreds and thousands of public opinions to make the city better. According to the *Zhejiang Online News*, the city's petition rate lowered nearly 50 percent one year after its establishment, forming a bridge between the citizens of Hangzhou and the local government.

In that spirit, the treasures of the city's natural landscape, historical sites, and cultural relics are beloved amongst the people who call Hangzhou home. Most of the city's older architectural achievements have maintained their original looks; for example, on Beishan and Nanshan roads, visitors will see old villas and houses owned by officials or wealthy families in the past—perhaps converted into shops and galleries—still with their original architectural features in place, consolidated but unchanged by the ages.

The volunteers in West Lake service spots provide free maps and tea, route guides, travel tips, and even take time out to help tourists design their tours while in Hangzhou. Quite apart from being helpful, these volunteers act as a sort of ad hoc petty police for the tourist sites throughout Hangzhou, reminding visitors to throw away their rubbish in the proper areas and not to damage the environment and public facilities.

There is much one might brag about their city—that it's big, that it's modern, that it's convenient—but, Hangzhou takes pride in the care and selflessness its citizens put into making Hangzhou a truly civilized city.

villa
花园住宅

convert
转变

consolidate
巩固

ad hoc
专门的

brag
吹嘘

Staying Centered and Keeping Fit

soothe
抚慰

meditative
冥想的

indulge
享受

chuiwan
捶丸

If Hangzhou's known for one thing, it's peace and quiet. For those looking to work either on their inner self or on their body, Hangzhou provides a variety of options for every traveler. If it's your mind you're looking to soothe, you can spend time taking meditative walks, bike through ancient city streets, pick up a good book, or relax in luxury in a spa. For the body, you might want to get in some long distance running to prepare for Hangzhou's annual marathon, or perhaps you could slow things down a bit with some golf. Whether you're taking in some tai chi or indulging in the city's TCM specialties, Hangzhou will keep your mind and your body in good condition.

Golf in Hangzhou? Of Course!

Whilst it is generally believed that golf began life in Scotland during the Middle Ages, readers might be surprised to learn that *chuiwan*, a Mandarin phrase that literally means "ball hitting," was played in ancient China and very much resembles the modern game of golf so widely loved today. It has even been suggested that the game was in fact exported to Europe via Mongolian travelers.

Still skeptical? The rules for *chuiwan* are apparently very similar to those of modern golf. The popularity of the game was at its highest during the Song Dynasty, and Emperor Huizong himself was apparently a very keen golf enthusiast. Wherever golf first originated, it is a sport that has become increasingly popular throughout China, and in Hangzhou, one of the best destinations to head to for golf is undoubtedly the West Lake International Golf and Country Club.

Designed by Jack Nicklaus and operating since 1998, the course boasts wonderful scenery and great terrain for all degrees of expertise. Visitors are welcome every day of the week, and, as with any reputable golfing establishment, facilities include clubhouse, locker rooms, pro shop, restaurant, and bar. Also, don't worry about carrying clubs around because golf carts are always ready.

---

skeptical
心存疑惑的

terrain
地形

pro shop
球具店

club
球杆

in the running
有赢的希望

home ground
主场

Hangzhou Marathon: Definitely in the Running

Anyone who lives in Zhejiang and enjoys long-distance running will almost certainly have heard of the annual Hangzhou Marathon. Indeed, this race is one of the most famous marathons in China, and surely one of the most scenic routes for city running in the world.

First taking place in 1987, the marathon proved hugely popular, with over 30,000 people registering to take part in 2015, the highest number of participants ever recorded. But it is not just the numbers that are significant; it's also the scope of the participation that's impressive. There were 45 different countries represented in the race that took place in 2015. Course highlights including West Lake, the tea gardens, and the Qiantang River. Runners will be happy to know that the marathon takes place in November, when the conditions and climate prove a lot more comfortable.

Come on You Green Giants

Hangzhou Greentown Football Club is a top-level team in the Chinese Super League. The club's home ground is

Dragon Sports Center, possessing a more than respectable capacity of over 50,000. Why has Hangzhou's football team been dubbed "Greentown?" Aside from fitting the lush greenery of the city, the club's main investor is Greentown China Holdings Limited, owned by the savvy billionaire real estate magnate Song Weiping.

A key turning point was the purchase of the first team of Jilin Aodong in November of 2000, including their league position in the second division, for a reported total of 25 million RMB. From here on the club made slow but steady progress, finally achieving a promotion to the top tier when they finished runners-up in the 2006 season. Whilst Hangzhou Greentown have not yet become a big-name Chinese team, their highest ever league position being fourth in 2010, they play a brand of neat passing football that can be very pleasing to the eye and have also won firm praise.

Never Tired of Tai Chi

There are two main reasons to practice tai chi. First of all, it is a discipline that can be employed as a means of self-defense. Second—and perhaps of most

magnate
巨头

the second division
二级联赛

tier
等级

runner-up
亚军

relevance
关联

well-being
安康

relevance here, given that Hangzhou is famously a peaceful city—tai chi is widely practiced due to its benefits to personal health.

For newbies, you might want to take a few classes to get you started. To take a more relaxed approach to tai chi, simply take advantage of the many spots around Hangzhou where enthusiasts practice in the open air, arguably the best way to experience it like the locals do. Dotted around West Lake, on any given day, it will soon become obvious that Chinese people will never tire of tai chi—performing wherever there is a flat surface.

The attraction of tai chi is based around its perceived contribution to individual well-being, relieving the effects of stress on both body and mind and providing a much-needed form of physical exercise. Furthermore, the meditative side of tai chi is also cited as a positive means to keeping good health.

Take It as Read

Charging around trying to take in as much as humanly possible when traveling is all very well. But sometimes it also pays to take off the tourist hat, give the feet a rest for a few hours, and get busy with some books. It's not just good for your soul, it's good for your soles. Whilst Hangzhou is of course home to one of the top universities in China, the capital of Zhejiang Province also boasts an enviable array of libraries and bookstores, so it's worthwhile to search out the best ones.

The Zhongshuge Bookstore is based in the Binjiang District of the city. Nestled in the busy commercial district of Star Avenue, it is near the Qiantang River. This incredible space is truly something to behold. For example, the first room, with its circular shelves, makes clever use of mirrors to create a feeling of expansiveness while the impressive children's pavilion provides a veritable playground for learning.

Visiting Hangzhou and not being a Mandarin speaker doesn't mean you have no books to read. In the Foreign Language Bookstore visitors will find

sole
脚掌

enviable
值得羡慕的

behold
注意

veritable
名副其实的

sniff at
嗤之以鼻

all-important
至关重要的

three stories of stories from traditional classics to modern titles, in both Chinese and English. You might want to take some time here to pick up a few recipe books, a must for tourists hoping to take a little Hangzhou cuisine with them.

Also worth considering is Boku Bookstore. While there is arguably a limited selection regarding English texts, purchasing a famous piece of literature for as little as 10 RMB is not to be sniffed at, so it's worth a look for the bargain-hunting book fans. There is also an area dedicated to children, offering art items, games, and toys, not to mention the all-important cafe on the first floor.

To join the Zhejiang Library all a customer needs is their passport and 150 RMB, and there is a fairly large selection of books in English, a great option for book lovers. But, for Hangzhou's premier library, you're going to want to check out the Hangzhou Public Library. Established in 1958, the library covers over 40,000 square meters and hosts more than 2,000,000 books with over 2,000 seats for reading. Another great thing to remember about the Hangzhou Public Library is that a great many cultural events, talks, and exhibitions are held here, so it's where visitors can read and experience the literary culture of Hangzhou.

Traditional Chinese Medicine in Hangzhou

Hangzhou has long played a vital role in China's bustling traditional Chinese medicine (TCM) world. The glorious TCM tradition of Hangzhou is personified by Hu Xueyan, the only member of the merchant class in the Qing Dynasty to be awarded a red-topped hat (a rank indicating an officer of second grade by the Qing imperial court), and one of the few people given the rare privilege by Empress Dowager Cixi to ride a horse in the Forbidden City.

Of the merchant's many ventures—including banks, pawnshops and philanthropic projects, his best-known contribution that still stands to this day is Hu Qing Yu Tang, a medicinal hall known then for its quality in medicine, ethical treatment of customers, and affordable healthcare services. Launched in 1874, Hu Qing Yu Tang is as well-known as the Tong Ren Tang medicinal hall in Beijing and has a greater sense of architectural authenticity. Since its establishment, Hu Qing Yu Tang has strictly followed the *Taiping Pharmacopeia*, an

personify
表现

pawnshop
当铺

philanthropic
慈善的

exhaustive 详尽的	exhaustive and authoritative collection of drug-making doctrines and codes of practice compiled in the Southern Song, making it the indisputable crown jewel in the arts of natural medicine in China.
authoritative 权威的	
doctrine 原则	
indisputable 不容置疑的	Today, Hu Qing Yu Tang is China's only state-level TCM museum. The TCM lobby gives visitors the intriguing feeling of having traveled back in time 300 years and is a trustworthy place for souvenir-seekers looking for authentic Chinese herbal medicines and tonics. For first-timers in Hangzhou, the greatest charm of the museum may be the fact that the antique establishment is still visited by locals on a daily basis, lining up for diagnoses and prescriptions just as in days of old, which may be the greatest comfort to the frustrations and sorrows of Hu in his later years. Other major TCM players in Hangzhou include Guang Xing Tang and Zhang Tong Tai, the latter best known for its ointment clinic. There are also a dozen lesser-known but equally respected TCM brands one can visit for a taste of the city's TCM splendor, such as the 100-year-old San Shen Tai, 160-year-old Tian Lu Tang, and Fu Tong Chun, first built in 1609.
crown jewel 最珍贵的部分	
tonic 补药	
diagnose 诊断	
prescription 处方	
ointment 药膏	

Appendix

Place Names 地名机构名对照表

A Liang Noodle Restaurant 阿良面馆

Binjiang District 滨江区

Bird Islet 鸟岛

Boku Bookstore 博库书城

CAA Art Museum 中国美术学院美术馆

Central Lake District 中心湖区

Chengdong Park 城东公园

China Academy of Art (CAA) 中国美术学院

China Academy of Art, Xiangshan Campus 中国美术学院象山校区

China National Silk Museum 中国丝绸博物馆

Chun'an County 淳安县

Dadou Road Food Street 大兜路美食街

Daqi Mountain National Forest Park 大奇山国家森林公园

Dong Yi Shun 东伊顺

Dragon Sports Center 黄龙体育中心

Forbidden City 紫禁城

Foreign Language Bookstore of Zhejiang Province 浙江省外文书店

Former Residence of Hu Xueyan 胡雪岩故居

Fu Tong Chun 傅同春

Fuchun River 富春江

Fuyang District 富阳区

Gan Qi Shi 甘其食

Gaoyin Street 高银街

Guang Xing Tang 广兴堂

Guangji Bridge 广济桥

Hangzhou Grand Theatre 杭州大剧院

Hangzhou Paradise 杭州乐园

Hangzhou Changqiao Polar Ocean Park 杭州长乔极地海洋公园

Hangzhou Public Library 杭州图书馆

Hangzhou Safari Park 杭州野生动物世界

Hangzhou Youth & Children's Park 杭州少儿公园

Hangzhou Zoo 杭州动物园

Hubin Qingyu 湖滨晴雨

Hu Qing Yu Tang 胡庆余堂

Huangfanr 皇饭儿

Huanglongdong Park 黄龙洞公园

Inna Art Space 清影艺术空间

Jing Yang Guan 景阳观

Jinhua City 金华市

Jiu Zhi Zhai 九芝斋

Kunshan City 昆山市

Lin'an 临安

Lin'an District 临安区

Longmen Ancient Town 龙门古镇

Manjuelong Village 满觉陇村

Meifeng Peak 梅峰

Moonlight Scenic Area 月光岛景区

Pan Tianshou Memorial 潘天寿纪念馆

Qiandao Lake 千岛湖

Qiantang River 钱塘江

Qinghefang (Hefang Street) 清河坊 (河坊街)

San Shen Tai 三慎泰

Shaoxing 绍兴

Sheng County 嵊州

Siberia 西伯利亚

Song Dynasty Town 宋城

Southern Song Imperial Street 南宋御街

Star Avenue 星光大道

Taiziwan Park (Prince Bay Park) 太子湾公园

Tangqi Town 塘栖镇

The Grand Canal 大运河

Tian Lu Tang 天禄堂

Tianmu Mountain 天目山

Tong Ren Tang 同仁堂

Tonglu County 桐庐县

Wanlong Ham House 万隆火腿庄

West Lake Cultural Plaza 西湖文化广场

West Lake International Golf and Country Club 西湖国际高尔夫球乡村俱乐部

West Lake Museum 西湖博物馆

Wushan Hill 吴山

Xianghu Lake 湘湖

Xiaoshan District 萧山区

Xiao Shao Xin 小绍欣

Xixi National Wetland Park (Xixi Wetlands) 西溪国家湿地公园 (西溪湿地)

Yan Ziling Fishing Platform 严子陵钓台

Yaolin Fairyland 瑶琳仙境

Temple of Yue Fei 岳飞庙

Yuhang District 余杭区

Zhang Tong Tai 张同泰

Zhejiang Art Museum 浙江美术馆

Zhejiang Library 浙江图书馆

Zhejiang Museum of Natural History 浙江自然博物馆

Zhi Wei Guan 知味观

Zhongshuge Bookstore 钟书阁

Names of Important Figures 人名对照表

Bai Juyi 白居易

Du Liniang 杜丽娘

Emperor Huizong of the Song Dynasty 宋徽宗

Emperor Qianlong 乾隆皇帝

Empress Dowager Cixi 慈禧太后

Feng Zikai 丰子恺

Hu Xueyan 胡雪岩

Huang Binhong 黄宾虹

Kitaro 喜多郎

Jack Nicklaus 杰克·尼克劳斯

Li Yu 李渔

Lin Bu 林逋

Lin Hong 林洪

Lin Sheng 林升

Liu Mengmei 柳梦梅

Marco Polo 马可·波罗

Nixon 尼克松

Pan Tianshou 潘天寿

Shou Daqing 寿达清

Song Weiping 宋卫平

Su Shi (Dongpo Jushi) 苏轼（东坡居士）

Sun Quan 孙权

Tang Xianzu 汤显祖

Wang Shu 王澍

Wu Changshuo 吴昌硕

Wu Zimu 吴自牧

Xishi (Xizi) 西施（西子）

Yu Qian 于谦

Yuan Mei 袁枚

Yue Fei 岳飞

Zhang Daqian 张大千

Zhang Yimou 张艺谋

Zhou Enlai 周恩来

Zong Ze 宗泽

Books, Operas, and Etc. 书籍剧目等对照表

A Record of the Millet Dream 《梦梁录》

Butterfly Lovers 《梁祝》

Compendium of Materia Medica 《本草纲目》

Dream of the Red Chamber 《红楼梦》

Impression West Lake《印象西湖》

Legend of the White Snake《白蛇传》

Menu of Sui Garden《随园食单》

Peach Blossom Fan《桃花扇》

Pure Supplies of the Mountain People
《山家清供》

Qianjiang Evening Post《钱江晚报》

Romance of the Song Dynasty
《宋城千古情》

Taiping Pharmacopeia
《太平惠民和剂局方》

The Peony Pavilion《牡丹亭》

The Story of the Western Wing
《西厢记》

Zhejiang Daily《浙江日报》

Zhejiang Online News《浙江在线》

Hangzhou Dishes 菜名对照表

beggar's chicken 叫花鸡

black crab in egg yolk 蛋黄青蟹

chrysanthemum cake 菊花糕

crunchy sesame candy 芝麻酥糖

dingsheng cake 定胜糕

Dongpo pork 东坡肉

fried eel noodles 鳝爆面

green bean cake 绿豆糕

hot rice in soup, *paofan* 泡饭

immortal duck and ham 火踵神仙鸭

Longjing shrimp 龙井虾仁

osmanthus jelly cake 桂花水晶糕

moon cake 月饼

pork with preserved vegetables 梅干菜扣肉

scone with sweet fermented rice wine
酒酿饼

small steam-basket buns, *xiaolongbao*
小笼包

stinky tofu with minced pork
肉末臭豆腐

West Lake carp in sweet and sour sauce
西湖醋鱼

A HOME IN HANGZHOU

图书在版编目(CIP)数据

杭州一瞥：精编版.心灵家园：英文 / 蒋景阳主编；吴昌提,盛湘君编. — 北京：商务印书馆,2023
ISBN 978-7-100-22540-3

Ⅰ.①杭… Ⅱ.①蒋… ②吴… ③盛… Ⅲ.①英语—语言读物 ②旅游指南—杭州—英文 Ⅳ.①H319.4：K

中国国家版本馆CIP数据核字(2023)第102975号

权利保留，侵权必究。

杭州一瞥：精编版

蒋景阳 主编

商 务 印 书 馆 出 版
(北京王府井大街36号 邮政编码100710)
商 务 印 书 馆 发 行
北京博海升彩色印刷有限公司印刷
ISBN 978-7-100-22540-3

2023 年 7 月第 1 版	开本 889×1194 1/32
2023 年 7 月第 1 次印刷	印张 7

定价：98.00 元